MY FIRST BOOK
GERMANY

ALL ABOUT GERMANY FOR KIDS

GLOBED
CHILDREN BOOKS

Interior and cover Design: Daniel Day
Editor: Margaret Bam

For My Sons, Daniel, David and Jude

Cologne, Germany

Germany

Germany is a **country**.

A country is land that is controlled by a **single government**. Countries are also called **nations, states, or nation-states**.

Countries can be **different sizes**. Some countries are big and others are small.

Neuschwanstein Castle, Germany

Where Is Germany?

Germany is located in the continent of **Europe**.

A continent is **a massive area of land that is separated from others by water or other natural features**.

Germany is situated in the western part of Europe.

Berlin Cathedral, Germany

Capital

The capital of Germany is Berlin.

Berlin is located in the **eastern part** of the country.

Berlin is the largest city in Germany.

Rostock, Germany

States

Germany is a country that is made up of 16 states.

The states of Germany are as follows:

Schleswig-Holstein, Hamburg, Mecklenburg-Vorpommern, Bremen, Brandenburg, Berlin, Niedersachsen, Sachsen-Anhalt, Sachsen, Thüringen, Hessen, Nordrhein-Westfalen, Rheinland-Pfalz, Saarland, Baden-Württemberg and Bayern.

German child

Population

Germany has population of around **84 million people** making it the 17th most populated country in the world and the 2nd most populated country in Europe.

Size

Germany is **357114 square kilometres** making it the 7th largest country in Europe by area.

Germany is the 63rd largest country in the world.

Languages

The official language of Germany is **German**. The German language originated in Germany and is now spoken by millions of people across the world.

Sorbian and North Frisian are also spoken in Germany.

Here are a few German phrases
- **Wie geht es dir?** - How are you?
- **Guten Tag** - Good morning

Brandenburg Gate, Germany

Attractions

There are lots of interesting places to see in Germany.

Some beautiful places to visit in Germany are

- **Berlin's Brandenburg Gate**
- **Cologne Cathedral (Kölner Dom)**
- **The Ultimate Fairytale Castle: Neuschwanstein**
- **The Black Forest**

Cologne, Germany

History of Germany

People have lived in Germany for a very long time, in fact ancient humans were present in Germany at least 600,000 years ago.

Adolf Hitler became the dictator of Germany from 1933 until his death in 1945. He rose to power as the leader of the Nazi Party.

Germany joined the European Union on 1st January 1958.

Oktoberfest Festival in Munich, Germany

Customs in Germany

Germany has many fascinating customs and traditions.

- German people are very hospitable and sociable. Many Germans have 'Kaffee und Kuchen', whereby families and friends stop working to come together in the afternoon for coffee and cake.
- A major festival in Germany is called Oktoberfest. This is an annual Munich Beer Festival and an important tradition.

Johann Sebastian Bach (1685-1750)

Music of Germany

There are many different music genres in Germany such as **Schlager music, Neue Deutsche Welle, Neue Deutsche Härte, Alpine folk music and Krautrock.**

Some notable German musicians include
- **Herbert Grönemeyer**
- **Nena Lena Meyer-Landrut**
- **Johann Sebastian Bach**
- **Rammstein**
- **Hans Zimmer**

Sauerbraten

Food of Germany

Germany is known for having delicious, flavoursome and rich dishes.

The national dish of Germany is **Sauerbraten** which is a traditional German roast of heavily marinated meat.

Food of Germany

Some popular dishes in Germany include

- **Königsberger klopse**
- **Maultaschen**
- **Labskaus**
- **Sausages**
- **Currywurst**
- **Döner kebab**
- **Schnitzel**
- **Käsespätzle**

Schiltach, Germany

Weather in Germany

Germany has a **temperate climate** characterised with warm summers and cold winters.

The warmest months in Germany are **July and August.**

Cows in Germany

Animals of Germany

There are many wonderful animals in Germany.

Here are some animals that live in Germany

- European Wildcat
- Wild Boar
- European Badger
- Bicolored Shrew
- Greater Horseshoe Bat
- Red Fox
- Wolves

Wasserkuppe, Germany

Mountains

There are many beautiful mountains in Germany which is one of the reasons why so many people visit this beautiful country every year.

Here are some of Germany's mountains

- Zugspitze
- Brocken
- Feldberg
- Wasserkuppe
- Wank

German football fan

Sports of Germany

Sports play an integral part in German culture. The most popular sport is Football.

Here are some of famous sportspeople from Germany

- **Michael Schumacher - Formula one**
- **Sebastian Vettel - Formula One**
- **Steffi Graf - Tennis**
- **Dirk Nowitzki - Basketball**

Ludwig van Beethoven (1770-1827)

Famous

Many successful people hail from Germany.

Here are some notable German figures

- **Otto von Bismarck - Chancellor**
- **Albert Einstein - Scientist**
- **Johannes Gutenberb - Inventor**
- **Ludwig van Beethoven - Composer**

Hamburg, Weihnachtsmarkt, Germany

Something Extra...

As a little something extra, we are going to share some lesser known facts about Germany.

- **65% of the highways in Germany have no speed limit.**
- **Germany is one of the largest car producers in the world.**

Words From the Author

We hope that you enjoyed learning about the wonderful country of Germany.

Germany is a country rich in culture and beauty, with lots of wonderful places to visit and people to meet.

We hope you continue to learn more about this wonderful nation. If you enjoyed this book, consider leaving a review!

With Love

15780267R00029